Is a Pharmaceutical Sales Career Right For Me?

To order additional copies of this book, contact:
Xlibris Corporation
1-888-795-4274
www.Xlibris.com
Orders@Xlibris.com
86233

Contents

Introduction: *The Career, The Industry* 7

1: *Closing the Gap* 11

2: *Probing and Persuading, with Principles* 22

3: *Right People, Right Communications,
   Right Action* 34

4: *Decide, Discover, Deliver: Instigators and
   Decision-Making Machines* 42

5: *Is Your Hair On Fire? Technical Ability,
   Professional Knowledge, On-Going Learning* 51

6: *Greatness: Tenacity, Adaptability, Resiliency* 59

7: *Conclusion and Self-Test* 67

8: *Acknowledgements and Further Reading* 72

About the Author

Carl Schott has successfully navigated three career changes over the past 30 years. His essential vision? Career moves are often possible and even advisable if the new career requires the same GENIUS (according to Webster "the peculiar structure of mind with which an individual is endowed . . .") that brought success in prior endeavors.

Driven at an early age to intellectual pursuits, Carl obtained his Ph.D. degree from the University of Notre Dame. During the Vietnam War era he served as an Army Officer, ultimately becoming a Strategic Intelligence Analyst in the Office of the Chief of Staff for Intelligence at the Pentagon.

Captivated by his first experience of leadership and management in the military, he entered the business world in New York City and had a successful career in merchandising and management with Bloomingdale's, Lord & Taylor, and Mitchells. As Store Manager of the prestigious Mitchells of Westport CT, and as Operating Vice-President and Managing Director within the Lord & Taylor system, Carl developed skills that later propelled his pharmaceutical sales and management career.

In 1992, after evaluating the costs to their family of continued big city life, Carl and his wife Ilona moved to Pennsylvania in a classic "Green Acres" migration and entered the pharmaceutical industry. Within three years, he became G.D. Searle's National "Rep of the Year" and moved back into Management as a District Sales Manager. Following the merger of Searle with the Pharmacia & Upjohn Company, Carl helped pioneer the position of Regional Staffing Manager. He was responsible for the recruitment, screening and placement of candidates in sales and management positions covering a seven state area and the District of Columbia. In his staffing assignment, he interviewed more than 3000 candidates. Of these, 175 were hired by his company and more than 98% of them were still successful in the field two years later when his company was acquired by Pfizer.

About the Author

Carl then joined Inventivhealth in that company's premier pharmaceutical recruiting organization and in just four years, placed 700 candidates in Florida and Puerto Rico alone. Many of them completed this workbook before interviewing successfully.

Carl's passion for helping people navigate through their own "changes" prompted him to form Schott Associates, Inc. In this role, Carl is a servant-leader in the Pharmaceutical recruiting industry, helping candidates and clients realize their professional goals.

Introduction

Introduction:
A Workbook for Candidates

This workbook is NOT JUST a "How-To" book on getting a job in the field of Pharmaceutical Sales. In that interest, it will make you a better prepared and better qualified candidate.

This workbook IS the product of unprecedented investigation into the recruitment process designed to uncover the ideal "fit" between candidate and client.

A few years ago, I had the GREAT opportunity to help design a Staffing Manager function for a major pharmaceutical company. Countless hours were spent working with consultants and focus groups of reps, managers and hiring professionals. The end product was a unique, trend-setting screening and staffing system. Subsequently, with the recruiting arm of Inventihealth, I continued to refine and deepen my insight into what makes a successful candidate.

BOTH POSITIONS PROVIDED THE RIGHT MARRIAGE OF CANDIDATE AND CLIENT—the type of ideal connection that can only come from the melding of candidate aspirations and corporate goals.

So, here's the key question. WHO SHOULD READ THIS WORKBOOK? It is intended to guide candidates who are considering a career change into deep contemplation of their true motives and ultimate suitability for this type of career/marriage. Hopefully, it will deter poorly-suited candidates and entice the best-suited ones.

The CAREER

Pharmaceutical Sales is the most rewarding area of endeavor you will ever enjoy. However, it is not a world of unrelenting bliss. In the past few years, many pharmaceutical companies have downsized their sales forces in what has been a major transition for the industry. As a result, the expectations companies have for their remaining representatives and their new representatives are even greater. This workbook depicts the REAL

Introduction:
A Workbook for Candidates

challenges of the Pharmaceutical Sales career. Candidates are obviously lured by the blatant attractions of the job—dealing with sophisticated customers, selling life-saving products, earning an attractive base salary, lucrative incentive programs, a company car (or allowance), full benefits, and the fellowship of like-minded professionals.

Some candidates are attracted by phantasms—the "flexibility" of not having to punch a clock everyday, the "autonomy" of owning your own territory, the "respect' that comes from being a universally respected professional in a sophisticated sales arena. In the case of the IDEAL candidate, these "phantasms" take form and become the REALITY. For the wrong candidate, who took a course on the "100 Top Interview Questions in the Pharmaceutical Field" and were hired, this probably won't happen.

In a nutshell, the pharmaceutical sales career is vastly rewarding, but it requires a great deal of hard work, long hours, and real dedication. In the RIGHT marriage, all of these aspects are a joy!

THE INDUSTRY

Pharmaceuticals companies are in the news every day. Over the past twenty years, the industry as a whole showed remarkable growth. In the past decade, prescription drugs have *literally* become household words. Consider the number of commercials per hour on TV! The drug industry is certainly healthy.

In today's political climate, what is called "big pharma" is under increasingly intense scrutiny. With tighter regulation and this scrutiny, came the rightsizing and change in the role of the representative.

As with other industries today, there is increasing consolidation. Mergers and acquisitions sometimes dominate the news. At the same time, with advances in genomic research, small biotech firms continue

Introduction:
A Workbook for Candidates

to pop up. All of these developments present excellent opportunities for rewarding careers.

Overall, a key word for candidates to consider in evaluating individual employers in this industry is the "Pipeline"—how many products are on the horizon that will be marketed and sold in the near future? Another factor is what some analysts call the "Freshness Index"—how much patent life is left on the products currently promoted?

GUIDELINES FOR USE

As with any workbook, this one is only as good as YOUR serious input. It is not meant to be finished in one sitting. Rather each chapter and the exercises included should be done with honesty and seriousness of purpose. I guarantee that if you approach it with an open mind and heart, you will uncover hidden qualities, experiences, and aspirations.

Is a Pharmaceutical Sales Career Right for Me? You be the judge.

Closing the Gap

Chapter 1:
Closing the Gap

Pharmaceutical Sales can either be the easiest job you have ever hated, or the hardest job you have ever loved. Everything depends upon YOU and what you invest in the career. Regardless of your personal style or dominant personality "type," you can be successful in this field. Countless personalities have enjoyed medical sales success—analytical "geeks," hard core "closers," amiable "good ole boys," and the "showboats" who live for an audience and its approval. In any company, *all of them* can be found near the top of the heap.

As a candidate, you must know that the hiring company also faces a difficult challenge in evaluating you. A candidate's impact and communication strength as well as innate charisma all come to the fore in an interview. The curtains part and you're on stage for your big scene. You've prepared, studied the company, understand the market, dressed in your best navy suit, and got the second fresh haircut in two weeks. ENERGY! DRIVE! DETERMINATION! CHARM! APPLAUSE!

The problem is that a "coached" candidate, not necessarily suited for the position, can seldom maintain this level of intensity over the long haul in the day-to-day grind of business. The company info and recruitment brochures as well as the available workbooks on how to answer interview questions and get the job at best only *allude to* the challenges of this position. They cannot begin to show what day-to-day work will require.

Therefore, for you as a candidate, there are three important decisions to make: "Do I really want THIS career?" Next, "Am I selling the "real me" to get this position?" The third question is "Are my prior successes relevant to this career, *as well as* to my sense of what is really important in my life?" If you can answer "YES" to all three of these questions after completing *Chapter One* of this workbook, then I would encourage you to go on to the next sections in a real hurry.

Chapter 1:
Closing the Gap

If your answer to these questions is "No," spend some time in true contemplation of what your life and your career are all about before jumping ship. Are you ready to take the challenge? Here goes!

WHAT DRIVES YOU?

What makes you get out of bed every morning with a smile? What rings your chimes? What are you most proud of in your life? What would you never give up?

These types of introspective questions will be the core of this first series of exercises—the longest and most critical in this workbook. Pharmaceutical Sales requires both *real enthusiasm* for the PRODUCT *and* the PROCESS of selling them. If you are not true to yourself in the PROCESS, you will not have the COMMITMENT to the job that will carry you through the hard times. You will also not enjoy as deeply the sweetness of victory that comes frequently to the successful representative.

Once again, the first step is for *YOU* to evaluate *YOU*! To do so, I will help you deeply and honestly consider three areas.

1. What defines your character, hereafter called your "*GENIUS?*"
2. What can you do better than anybody you know, hereafter called your "*ABILITIES?*"
3. What do you REALLY care about, hereafter called your "*PASSIONS?*"

Throughout chapter one, we'll do some serious GAP (GENIUS, ABILITIES, PASSIONS) analysis and by the end of the workbook, hopefully *close the GAP* between you, success, and happiness.

Chapter 1:
Closing the Gap

FIRST, LET'S TAKE INVENTORY.

What is your GENIUS? The ancient Romans used this term to describe a guardian spirit believed to be assigned to each person at birth. In time, the term evolved to describe the peculiar structure of "mind" of an individual. Whether it's mind, soul, spirit—the bottom line is, your GENIUS is your footprint.

Consider the following lists of descriptors for what may be your GENIUS. They all relate to success in the medical sales profession:

Instigator	Listener
Goal—Setter	Problem Solver
Service Provider	Numbers Cruncher
Decision-Maker	Team Player
"Shot at the Buzzer Maker"	Counselor
Chameleon	Stickler for Detail
Logician	Persuader
Idea Broker	Matchmaker
Implementer	Person of Integrity
Innovator	Conscience of the Group
Intellectual sponge	Self-Starter
Natural Leader	Mediator
Worker bee	Detective

Right now, pick the top 5 that describe your GENIUS. Remember, pick the ones that most accurately describe who you think you really ARE. DO *NOT* pick those you *THINK* an employer is seeking. Do NOT pick those you think you CAN BE. *HONESTLY* evaluate what you bring to everything you do. Remember, you are the only person seeing or "grading" this exercise.

Chapter 1:
Closing the Gap

You will refer to these aspects of your GENIUS throughout this workbook. Again, all of these are visible and important in pharmaceutical sales representatives. The right combination produces the top performers.

Along with GENIUS come ABILITIES

Your ABILITIES are tools you have developed that help you impress your GENIUS upon the world. The list below includes many that are important in the field of Pharmaceutical Sales.

Your GENIUS is not an acquired trait or something easily learned by conscious effort. ABILITIES *CAN* be learned or acquired by conscious effort.

Here is a list of useful ABILITIES:

Time Management	Coaching
Extemporaneous Speaking	Strategic Planning
Use of Analytical	Tools Sales
Teambuilding	Teaching Ability
Money Management	Scheduling
Customer Service	Increasing Productivity
Motivating Others	Product Knowledge
Planning	Report Writing
Foreign Languages	Computer Skills
Accounting Skills	Negotiating Skills
Consulting Skills	Research/Data Gathering
Analytical Ability	Presentation Skills
Insert your Own here _____	

Chapter 1:
Closing the Gap

As with your GENIUS elements, list what you consider to be your top five ABILITIES:

_____

_____

_____

_____

_____

What matters most are your PASSIONS.

This is the part that will *drive* your personal analysis. PASSIONS are where your body and mind meet! PASSIONS are beliefs gone wild! PASSIONS are forces that drive you, inspire you, give you superhuman energy, pump up the adrenalin, ring your chimes! PASSIONS are intimately tied to your ideas AND feelings about yourself and your world. Your true PASSIONS live very near the core of your GENIUS. In fact, they're always just outside THE door, knocking softly, and sometime ringing the bell persistently.

PASSIONS are in themselves the personal "must haves" that are most meaningful to you. You must choose a career which requires these PASSIONS, reinforces your GENIUS, and maximizes the ABILITIES you have listed above. Without that three-fold mix, you're doomed to another probably ill-advised career change. *With* all three, you will enjoy each day the privilege of a lifetime—being who you are!

Here is a limited list of PASSIONS. Feel Free to add some of your own.

Recognition	Education	Money
Freedom	Family	Activity Fitness
Affiliation	Power	Leadership
Independence	Belonging	Charity

Chapter 1:
Closing the Gap

Physical Activity	Honesty	Problem Solving
Structure	Security	Leisure Time
Creativity	Variety	Spirituality
Success	Career Advancement	Safety

Now, as with GENIUS descriptors and ABILITIES, pick five of the PASSIONS including the ones I may not have listed since I've not had the pleasure of knowing YOU.

_____

_____

_____

_____

_____

So what do I do with all this information?

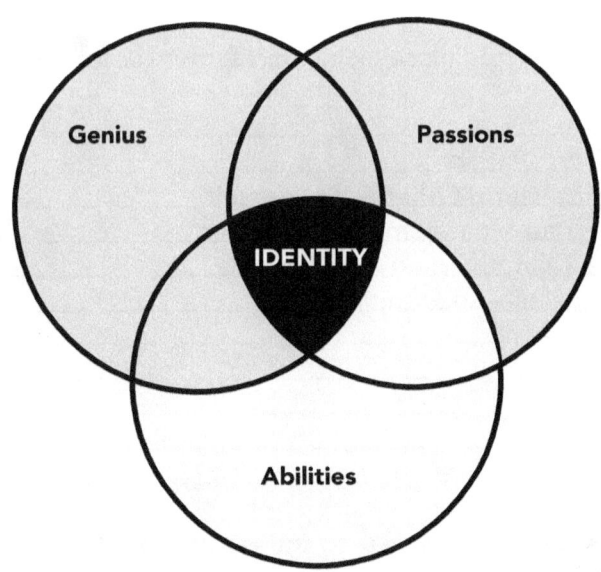

Chapter 1:
Closing the Gap

If you've been honest with yourself, you have all the data you need to make a life-changing decision. List your 15 chosen items below.

GENIUS	PASSIONS	ABILITIES

Study them carefully. Look for relationships. *Draw lines* between those that in your mind are most closely related. In doing so, you will begin to "close some GAPs"—creating the foundation for the chapters that follow.

When you've connected these elements, list them as follows. For example:

Genius—Ability—Passion
Instigator—Motivating Others—Leadership
Self Starter—Time Management—Structure
Team Player—Team Building—Affiliation
Idea Broker—Sales—Recognition

The variables are endless—as countless as the stars, but they form your unique IDENTITY.

Chapter 1:
Closing the Gap

Establish your IDENTITY

When you look at your choices, focus on the PASSION first. While the sales position requires many ABILITIES, the day to day grind of rejection and frustration requires a special set of PASSIONS. As you work through the book, consider how you FEEL about the situations you will be asked to confront.

LET'S JUMP THE FIRST GAP

To get started, recall five successes in your life that make you burst with pride. These must be things you *actually* did, NOT things you wish you had done. We're not looking at good interview stories here, but *real* chest-expanding, back-slapping SUCCESSES. Once again, nobody but you will ever see this, so be honest. List the five and write a brief description of them.

_____

_____

_____

_____

_____

Now the hard part: Take a look at each of these successes and decide which COMBINATIONS OF GENIUS, ABILITIES, AND PASSIONS made them possible.

AUTHOR'S NOTE TO PROSPECTIVE CANDIDATES: The sad news is that most candidates spend their interview time talking about their business accomplishments. Most do not verbally relate them to their ABILITIES, only occasionally talk about their GENIUS, and seldom coincidentally mention their PASSIONS. Their accomplishments ironically are usually *customized* for the interview situation. Their

Chapter 1:
Closing the Gap

prospective manager, therefore, hires the "phantasm" which was skillfully created for the interview, and only *later* meets the REAL person, whose PASSIONS, GENIUS and ABILITY then explode, for better or worse, into the workplace.

Conclusions, Disclaimers, Post-Mortems

Once again, this is NOT JUST a workbook designed to help you prepare for an interview. When it does, we have a "Win-Win!" It is intended to help you make a very important life choice. THE ONE THING OF WHICH I AM ABSOLUTELY AND UNEQUIVOCALLY CERTAIN IS THIS! What employers in Pharmaceutical Sales want are sales people who have the "fire in the belly" that it takes to be outstanding. That fire, that drive, CAN ONLY come from work that fulfills you and helps you to become *on a daily basis*, the person you really are. As Jack Mitchell, CEO of Mitchells/Richards consistently affirms, "you can't have two philosophies, one for your life and one for your business." Without that solid IDENTITY, you can *probably* survive in the business. But of course, the superstars are far more than "survivors" in any field.

What about Pharmaceutical Sales?

You're on the right track so far if your GENIUS, ABILITIES, AND PASSIONS point to the following areas:

    Salesmanship and Persuasiveness
    Teamwork and Collaboration
    Tenacity and Adaptability (ironically, both at the same time)
    Customer Focus and Impact
    Technical Knowledge and Continuous Learning

If they do, let's go ahead. In the coming chapters we will look at the Pharmaceutical Sales Career as it really IS.

Chapter 1:
Closing the Gap

One last thought on "closing the GAP"—

> "Consider a bit of advice given to a young Native American
> At the time of his initiation:
>
> As you go the way of life, you will see a great chasm.
>
> Jump.
>
> It is not as wide as you think."
>
> —Joseph Campbell

Probing and Persuading,
with Principles

Chapter 2:
Probing and Persuading, with Principles

"Each Company's search for value, and each individual's search for identity will change the corporate landscape forever".

—Marcus Buckingham and Curt Coffman.
First Break All the Rules.

It should be clear by now that a career change must essentially be a confirmation of your IDENTITY. What will your identity be as a representative? THE ANSWER IS PROFOUNDLY SIMPLE! Your business cards will say it all—(insert name) "Medical *Sales* Representative." It will not say "Medical Diplomat," "Medical Counselor," "Teacher," "Coach," "Friend" etc. Sure, you will need to be all of those, but in essence you are a *salesperson*.

Now that you have your personal inventory in order, let's consider how it relates to the field of Pharmaceutical Sales. During the past seven years, as a District Sales Manager, Regional Staffing Manager, and Professional Recruiter, I have interviewed over 9,000 candidates in person or by phone. Of these just less than 10% were hired by our company. I *must* believe that the other 90% thought they could succeed in the Pharmaceutical Industry. But many serious candidates had *no clue* about the realities of pharmaceutical sales even at late stages of the interview process. Even worse, *and more numerous* were those who had friends who were surviving in the industry, working 10-3 under inadequate supervision, and spending their afternoons at the gym or watching Oprah! (no offense meant to Oprah!)

Face it, "drug reps" have gained a bit of notoriety over the past decade, from the sleazy vamp on *ER*, to significant exposure in MAXIM, to the real life contestants on some BIG reality TV shows (*Survivor, The Bachelor* etc.)—all potential models or actresses, all handsome or beautiful, all clever, all ambitious, and all goal-oriented.

Chapter 2:
Probing and Persuading,
with Principles

MUST *YOU* BE LIKE THESE PEOPLE TO REALLY SELL? MORE IMPORTANTLY, ARE THESE ATTRIBUTES ENOUGH TO MAKE YOU A SUCCESS?

At this point you may be tempted to say "Well, Pharmaceutical sales is not really sales anyway. It's more of an educational or marketing job." OR "Yes, but I've heard that Pharmaceutical Sales is different because you *don't have to close.*"

ALARM! DANGER!! MELTDOWN IN PROGRESS!! EVACUATE THE BUILDING!! *Say that to anybody in the industry on an interview and you may as well end the discussion!!!!*

Sales, pharmaceutical or otherwise, is sales!. Sales is sometimes tough. Sales is sometimes getting doors slammed in your face.

This is true to the "nth" degree. The recent changes in patient confidentiality rules have allowed more and more offices and institutions to almost forcibly exclude you from their confines—the easiest place to have contact with the doctor.

In addition, recent changes in governmental regulation (READ THE NEWS EVERY DAY) are making it more and more difficult for you to sell your branded innovative drugs. The anticipated new mandated Prescription Drug plan will solidly favor generic drugs. One recently approved Senate bill allows patients to import drugs at a reduced price from Canada. Managed Care plans running these programs will translate these regulations into more restrictions—you can be certain of that.

YOUR JOB AS A PHARMACEUTICAL REP GETS HARDER EVERY DAY!

Chapter 2:
Probing and Persuading,
with Principles

So what does this mean to you?

The pharmaceutical industry will always be driven by new patented products. Progress in medical care will depend on the new drugs that YOU will sell. Companies are spending a greater percentage of their profits on research and development to bring these new products to patients. Finally, the pharmaceutical industry has successfully faced all these types of challenges before and actually grown stronger. How? Primarily by the efforts of skillful and professional sales representatives.

What's happened to all the talk about PASSION?

Another simple answer . . . As you read on, you will see that if the scenarios we describe do not relate to your dominant IDENTITY, you will *not* succeed in this increasingly difficult, but vastly rewarding profession.

ONE MORE BIG DISCLAIMER—I'm not going to write yet another book on *how to sell*. Who could top Zig Ziglar and all his countless "edu-tainment" colleagues and imitators? The bottom line is this—you will be a salesperson, and in pharmaceutical sales, your Probing, Persuading, and Closing will not be for just an order. SOOOOO MUCH MORE THAN THAT!!! Your responsibility as a rep is to get a commitment to meaningful, repetitive *action*. EVEN MORE THAN THAT!!! THE PHARMACEUTICAL SALES CLOSE IS 100 TIMES HARDER THAN ANY YOU CAN IMAGINE, because your close is for a commitment by the physicians or medical professionals *to change the way they practice medicine.*

THINK ABOUT THAT!! Physicians must change the way the practice medicine in order to REALLY get started with your product.

Chapter 2:
Probing and Persuading, with Principles

Now do you understand what I meant about PASSION, doing a job that energized the core of your being, working on your ABILITIES, feeding the GENIUS that make you the person you are? Without these elements you might end up as what we call a "sample dropper" (free samples or "patient starters" are for many reps their most important "stock-in-trade"), a glorified "UPS" man, or a caterer who brings chocolate, donuts, even lunch to the office staff in exchange for a "Signature." If that turns you on, you may get hired, be mediocre, get bored, and ultimately move on to sales in another industry.

But if one of your PASSIONS is something like "being the best" in your field . . . read on!

THE PHARMACEUTICAL SALES PROCESS

Pharmaceutical Sales is a UNIQUE process. At the Primary Care level, the physician has many reasons *not* to make a decision to prescribe a new product. There are steps you must follow to make this conversion. The belief in the industry is that it takes five calls to make that happen. I would contend that it would take an infinite number of calls to change somebody's *modus operandi* if your message is just a presentation on every call. Your sales calls must include probing, presentation, persuasion, *closing*, and a continual demonstration of principle that builds trust.

There are at least four ABILITIES you need to develop:

1. Laser-like Uninterrupted Customer Focus
2. Persuasiveness
3. Ability to win Trust through demonstrating Integrity,
4. Ability to Close.

For each of these, I will list a series of exercises to help you understand how your pre-existing GENIUS, and PASSIONS relate to each of them.

Chapter 2:
Probing and Persuading,
with Principles

As in Chapter One, once you have finished, you will have a better understanding of whether Pharmaceutical Sales is right for you. GET READY TO WORK.

The Laser!

In pharmaceutical sales, your mission is complicated by the fact that *you do not sell to the customer*. WHAT?!? You heard me. In Pharmaceutical Sales you do not sell to the end user of your product—the patient. You sell to the physician, pharmacist, or hospital that prescribes your drug, recommending that the patient take it. Your doctors, nurses, pharmacists must stand in YOUR place when advising the patients. THEY are the diplomats, teachers, counselors, coaches, not you. YOU have to motivate them to fill those roles.

To do that, you have to understand *their* world. When I began my pharmaceutical sales career years ago my District Sales Manager advised me to "talk about patients, not pills." What that meant was that I had a few minutes in each call *to relate* my drug to the PATIENTS the physicians treated in their office every day.

The LASER is energized by two major skills—Probing and Listening.

As in chapter one, let's focus on your past experiences to see if you have what it takes to do that—whether you've been in sales before, whether you're a new college grad, whether you're a registered nurse, an auditor or project manager with Deloitte & Touche, or a salesman for Dad's Insurance Agency.

In this and each succeeding chapter, you will evaluate scenarios. I've avoided using only sales situations, since many of you have not really been sales professionals. Just the same, you can use sales, teaching, counseling, coaching, interpersonal and family experiences as models in answering these questions. As in Chapter One, think deeply and

Chapter 2:
Probing and Persuading,
with Principles

try to recall situations in which you faced a challenge, took steps to overcome it, and produced a result profitable or pleasant for both you and the person encountered. Once again, two of the three scenarios in each exercise will always relate to everyday situations. One will be drawn directly from the pharmaceutical sales profession. Let's consider your probing ABILITIES.

Here goes:

1. Describe the best detective work you've ever done to obtain information to better understand somebody else's actions? What did you do? What did you learn? What happened as a result to change your relationship?

2. Friends, customers, spouses—just about everybody you know—often make unreasonable demands. When did this happen to you most recently? What did you do? What did you learn? What happened as a result to change your relationship?

3. Pharmaceutical Scenario. You are making your first real sales call and your District Manager is with you. You're really pumped about your new product that was just launched. You ask to see Dr. Bliffstick. The receptionist, without taking the phone off her shoulder or her eyes off her computer monitor says, "Dr. Bliffstick *never* sees drug reps." At which point, like an apparition, a competing rep walks out into the patient waiting room from the "back." What do you do?

The obvious point about all of these situations is that they require you to *probe* and *listen* before taking action. If you did that in each of your answers to these challenges, move on.

Chapter 2:
Probing and Persuading, with Principles

PERSUASIVENESS

Some candidates who have been nurses and other clinicians say, "I've never sold"—to which I say, "BALONEY! You're selling all the time!" At their core, most interpersonal relationships require *persuasion*. How did you get a date for the prom? How did you get your parents to extend your curfew? How did you get your wife to let you buy that new sand wedge? All require persuasion and salesmanship.

Persuasiveness works on both an *intellectual* and *emotional* level. In the pharmaceutical industry, you "make your presentations" with *intellectual* tools—studies, articles, patient type overviews, etc. You "sell" with *emotion*.

Remember, medical professionals DO NOT change the way they practice medicine, the "standard of care" that was drummed into them during almost a decade of med school, internships, residencies, etc. *without* an emotional appeal. Something about what you say must ring true in the *deepest sense* to get this type of reaction.

So let's consider the art of persuasion and your ABILITIES.

1. What was the best idea you ever "sold" to a friend, spouse, boss, customer, professor? What did you do? What happened?

2. Have you ever been in a situation where you had to motivate others to take actions to support a corporate or even office reorganization or to undertake a family relocation, or to conduct an "intervention" to solve a loved-one's addiction or behavioral problem? How did you do it? What resulted?

3. Pharmaceutical Sales Example. Dr. Patel is very courteous on your first call with him. He allows you to make a full presentation,

Chapter 2:
Probing and Persuading, with Principles

and even asks the same questions they told you to expect in training. You WOWed him. At the end of the call, he says, "that's fine but I never use a new drug until it's been on the market for at least a full year." But YOU have to make your sales numbers THIS MONTH. How would you persuade him to CHANGE THE WAY HE PRACTICES MEDICINE?

BUILDING TRUST THROUGH INTEGRITY

The first pharmaceutical challenge above indicated that pharmaceutical sales is often frustrating due to *access* issues. Also, physicians and prescribers often see the world of prescription drugs as part of an "undifferentiated" market. When Primary Care Physicians deal with arthritis management, in their minds Celebrex==Mobic=traditional NSAIDs. In hyperlipidemia, Crestor=Lipitor=Simvastatin. Each physician selects a favorite drug, but will switch for no apparent reason to another product because he or she has been "sold" or because a few vocal patients were dissatisfied or because their managed care formulary changed. In addition, many physicians at first place *little value* on your input. *That's where the integrity issue is critical.*

I'LL EXPLAIN. In this environment, selling results from brevity and clarity. Most unproductive calls in a doctor's office begin with "Can I have two minutes of your time?" This is usually followed by a sigh, "I'm really swamped, just leave me some literature." Or "Let me sign for your samples. I've been using tons of (name your drug) lately!"

This approach is even less effective than the "Can I help you?" used all-too-commonly in retail stores. It just doesn't sell.

In pharmaceutical sales you have to GRAB your customer's attention with a strong opening statement, show them how your drug will be a

Chapter 2:
Probing and Persuading, with Principles

benefit to their practice, get them to take action, and then follow up on the results they experience.

If you get into the industry, your company will give you an FDA-approved sales presentation to master. Your Sales Managers will coach you on its delivery. You will in many cases be rated on how you do it in their presence. All of this is well and good. But it does not sell—YOU do!

What sells is your repeated, knee-to-knee contact with your Physicians, Pharmacists, Physician's Assistants, Nurse Practitioners and others about actions they took with the information you provided, and what resulted. Once they've tried your drug with favorable results, the gates open.

HOWEVER, the gates remain open only if your initial presentations and all of your follow up is *honest, accurate and consistent*. Exaggerate or lie *just once* to a physician who put his or her neck on the line to change the way he or she practices medicine as a result of your persuasion—and get caught at it—and the only thing you'll be selling is swampland in central Florida.

In the long run—and I hope you'll be in this for the long run—it's your *integrity* that makes you successful.

Consider the following three situations where your actions may help you demonstrate integrity.

1. You take a job interview on a work day. The interviewer asks how you got the time off from your job. What do you say?

2. Have you ever refused to sell something to a customer because you knew it did not meet their needs? What did you do? What happened?

Chapter 2:
Probing and Persuading,
with Principles

3. Pharmaceutical Sales Scenario. A physician is very happy with results he has achieved prescribing your drug. But somehow, he has the dosing wrong. He's actually doubling the indicated dosage of your pain drug. What do you do? How do you also keep his business?

As with the questions above, all of these situations indicate your basic interest in arriving at and promulgating the truth. If you never have done any of these . . . hmmmm . . . . Otherwise, move on.

CLOSING? IS YOUR CUSTOMER THE REARVIEW MIRROR?

In the pharmaceutical industry, Sales Ability is, bottom line, the ability to get prescriptions. You are paid on the prescriptions written by doctors in your territory. In the today's world, where physician time is limited, managed care and hospital formularies attempt to direct their prescribing habits, and the crunch of seeing 50-60 patients during their office days makes them irritable and aloof, you must do more than present and provide service (in the form of samples and patient education information—not to mention the chocolate, donuts, and lunches).

You must LEAD your customers as a conductor leads a symphony—the way a basketball coach shouts from the sidelines—the way a teacher implants ideas and actions into their students. Laser Focus is the first ability, but it is not enough. Probing and Listening are critical, but they are not enough. Presentation and Persuasion are critical, but they are not enough. Integrity and Trust are essential, but they are not enough. You have to CLOSE FOR ACTION.

As mentioned above, closing in sales is usually asking for a purchase order—getting the signature on the bottom line. In pharmaceutical sales, it is asking for a change in behavior. IF YOU DO REQUEST

Chapter 2:
Probing and Persuading, with Principles

SPECIFIC ACTION IN YOUR SALES CALLS, YOU WILL SUCCEED IN THIS BUSINESS!

George Colony, chief of Forrester Research has said "The customer is a rearview mirror, not a guide to the future." Physicians, more than most other professionals, work via a rearview mirror, looking back at what was drummed into them after all those sleepless nights in med school and internships. *You* have to lead them into the future—into the world of innovation and life-saving changes. YOUR CLOSES, AND ONLY YOUR CLOSES, ACCOMPLISH THIS.

When we get to the chapter on Planning and Organization, you will learn how to latch on to your top, cutting-edge, progressive targets like a lamprey eel onto a whale, like white on rice, like plain ole glue! But that's later.

Right now, you have to ask the key question *once again*. "How do I feel about this?" Just as managers often hire "from their gut," candidates should take jobs "from their gut." Does it FEEL right? If so, go on to the next chapter.

From here on out, the Chapters are a bit shorter and more simply focused on specific aspects of the pharmaceutical sales job. WHEW!

Right People, Right
Communications, Right Action

Chapter 3:
Right People,
Right Communications,
Right Action

Your GENIUS, ABILITIES, AND PASSION that enable you to sell will be challenged in pharmaceutical sales from two primary directions. Your *customers* are a constant challenge as you strive to change the way they act. In most pharmaceutical companies you *also* will face individual challenges as you learn to work and sell as part of a *team* of representatives.

In several different publications, Tom Peters emphasizes the rapid changes in our business environment by explaining that in 1970 "it took 108 guys some 5 days to unload a ship full of timber. And now? Container daze: Eight guys . . . one day(!!!)"

Companies (READ THE NEWS EVERY DAY) have used technology to help downsize, "rightsize," consolidate etc. to reduce payroll, garner economies of scale, work more efficiently. You as an individual are no different. How often do you use an ATM machine rather than a human teller? Do you pump your own gas? Wash your car at a gas station?

CONTRARY TO ALL THE APPARENT PREVAILING LAWS OF BUSINESS CHANGE, nearly all major pharmaceutical companies now have *multiple* teams of representatives in the same geographic territory often selling one or two of the same products. When I was a representative, I OWNED my territory. Then our company was preparing to launch a true "blockbuster" drug that you now see on TV every 15 minutes or so. We added a second and third team, while contracting with a well-known "rent-a-rep" company to augment our sales force. We went from 475 to about 775 reps in one year. The following year, we added another 750 or so and as we approached launch date, realized that to compete we needed to double again. We joined into a co-marketing agreement with a MAJOR power in the industry.

The goal was *frequency* of calls on key physicians and *reach* to a broader base of physician specialties. The goal was to dominate the physicians' time by winning what the industry calls "share of voice." To market blockbuster products it is critically important that companies reach the

Chapter 3:
Right People,
Right Communications,
Right Action

right physicians, with the right frequency, delivering the right message. During the past decade, the big players, Merck, Pfizer, Novartis, Astra-Zeneca and others all began creating multiple product teams. In addition, companies co-market their products with other companies to more or less "outsource" some of their efforts. Finally, as I just mentioned, whole companies exist that provide rep teams for a designated period of time to provide a more or less "instant" expansion.

Given the fact that physicians have less and less time to be sold to by sales reps, it became obvious that the bigger companies with the most recognizable products would gain the dominant "share of voice." Given the financial reports from these companies, it clearly works!

As a twenty-first century rep, you will coordinate constantly with your partners day-in, day out, rain or shine.

Don't forget the sales specialists.

Another aspect of planning and team-building comes from the fact that companies now have a variety of sales and clinical science specialists who are also active in each geographic area. There are often Hospital and/or Institutional Representatives calling on major hospitals. There are Managed Care specialists calling on the major managed care plans affecting your area. There are Key Account Specialists calling on Pharmacies and Wholesalers. There are Clinical Education Managers and Clinical Science Managers (usually PharmD's) also active in YOUR territory.

As a representative, your ability to plan your activities, augmented by all these other partners, is critical. In addition, your ability to work strategically with them is also *essential*. You're the one who has primary responsibility.

Remember, in most situations, your financial incentives are directly tied to the activities of ALL of these people.

Chapter 3:
Right People,
Right Communications,
Right Action

So what? The point is that in the majority of cases, the "lone wolf" sales representative in the pharmaceutical industry is a thing of the past—a dinosaur—GONE! You must now not only be a team player, but a team LEADER. You have to develop the ABILITIES to produce outstanding results in a team environment. Finally, *you have to convince your customers of the value added in working with a team of representatives.*

Sound weird, doesn't it? It's probably not what you expected. Let's see if you enjoy this environment.

PLANNING AND ORGANIZING

Be reassured, in pharmaceutical sales, you will *not* be given a phone book and told to go find doctors, pharmacies, and hospitals as clients. Nearly all pharmaceutical companies have detailed targeting plans, sorted by physician specialty or geography, designed to maximize the potential business in each territory. It is certain that if you succeed in gaining a pharmaceutical job, you will be given a target list that you will be expected to follow.

You will also be held responsible to uncover new opportunities as physicians and other prescribers move in and out of your territory. But the qualitative part of your annual review is influenced to a great degree by your ability to reach and convert the top targets on your assigned list.

Secondly, in dealing with your partners, you must lead the team in planning a call schedule or route. The worst scenario is that two or three reps with the same product end up in the same office on the same day. At best, two of three will not produce anything but ill will for "wasting" the office's time. At worst, all three will lose credibility for not being able to plan something as simple as a daily routing system.

Chapter 3:
Right People,
Right Communications,
Right Action

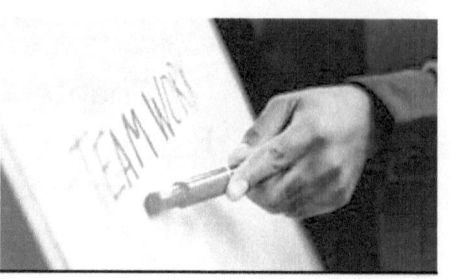

Remember you are living in a bi-polar world now! Your goal as a "sales professional" is to "set yourself apart" from the rest and establish a personal relationship with your customers. At the same time, you need to be part of a team. Believe me, it can and *must* be done. Just as great sports teams with no identifiable superstar often win championships, sales teams produce similar results.

Once again—does this FEEL right to you? Do you want to work in this world? Frankly, at this point, half of the straight commissioned, entrepreneurial sales folks working on this course may lose interest.

So be it! You're making the right choice—*for you!*

For the rest—let's move on! *Planning and organizing activities are essentially the process of establishing courses of action for yourself and others to make sure you get the job done effectively.*

Consider the following three "*Planning and Organizing*" cases.

1. In all walks of life we have priorities that do not always mesh with those of our associates, spouses, partners, friends. At times we even face conflicting priorities. When did this happen to you? What did you do? What resulted from the decisions you made? What would you do differently next time?

2. Sometimes the crush of daily events prevents us from really planning future activities. Think about a recent time when you could only react to an important challenge because you had not prepared. What happened? What did you learn? What would you do differently next time?

Chapter 3:
Right People,
Right Communications,
Right Action

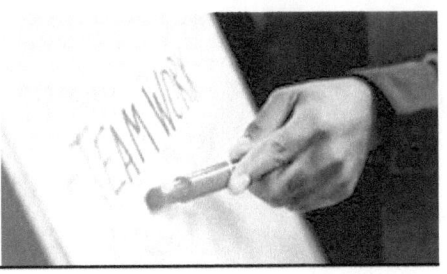

3. Pharmaceutical scenario. You've just spent your last budgeted expense dollars to buy lunch for major office of 30 employees to get to see three "no-see" physicians (those in the prior chapter who never "*SEE*" drug reps.) Two are very important and one is a new member of the staff, fresh out of Residency. Like the great caterer you are, you are busy in the office kitchen area when the Office Manager says, "Oh, I'm sorry you didn't call this morning to reconfirm. The doctors are having an important meeting and can't join us for lunch." What did you do wrong? What should you have done? What can you do to rescue the situation?

How should planning be executed? By building . . . .

STRATEGIC RELATIONSHIPS WITH CUSTOMERS AND TEAMMATES

Your relationship with your customers and your partners is not a friendship, although in the perfect world, I suppose, friendship will be a by-product. It is an integrated, targeted effort to achieve a goal by maximizing the inherent GENIUS and acquired ABILITIES fired by the PASSIONS of each team member. Maximizing team efforts relates obviously to the tasks of customer targeting and daily sales call routing. It can also relate to personalities. As mentioned in chapter one, physicians (they are human) all relate to different personality types in different ways. Your "zero" is somebody else's "super-customer."

You and your teammates must capitalize on your diversity in order to reach all the targets, not only with the right message and the right frequency, but also *with the right person from your team as lead horse.*

Let's look at three "Strategic Relationship" scenarios:

Chapter 3:
Right People,
Right Communications,
Right Action

1. Discuss your must successful technique for encouraging team members (family members, social group members) to contribute their unique talents to a project. What did you do? What was the result?

2. Discuss a time when you worked with a peer/spouse/teammate to determine roles and divide responsibilities? How did it go? What was the result?

3. Pharmaceutical Scenario. A new member has joined your team of associates to sell your #1 product to Primary Care Physicians. On a call with Dr. Cassandra, one of the top doctors, she tells you, "I never want to see that new rep from your company. She does not understand my practice, doesn't know her product well, and tried to strong-arm me into prescribing your drugs. I never want to see her again. In fact, I really only want to see *one* rep from your company—YOU!" What do you do? What do you tell Dr. Cassandra? What do you tell your new partner? What do you tell your boss?

All of these activities are *daily* occurrences in the Pharmaceutical sales arena. Are you still interested? Remember, this IS the pharmaceutical sales reality.

Chapter 3:
Right People,
Right Communications,
Right Action

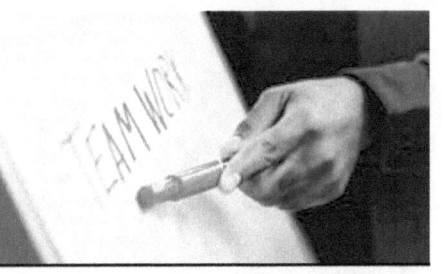

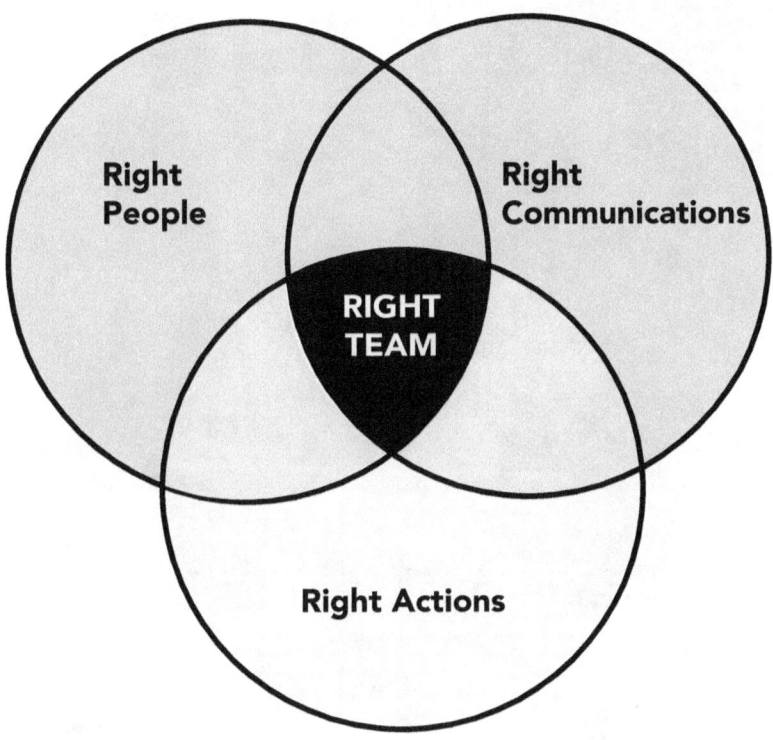

Now let's move on to "Decision Making/Initiating Action."

Instigators and
Decision-Making Machines

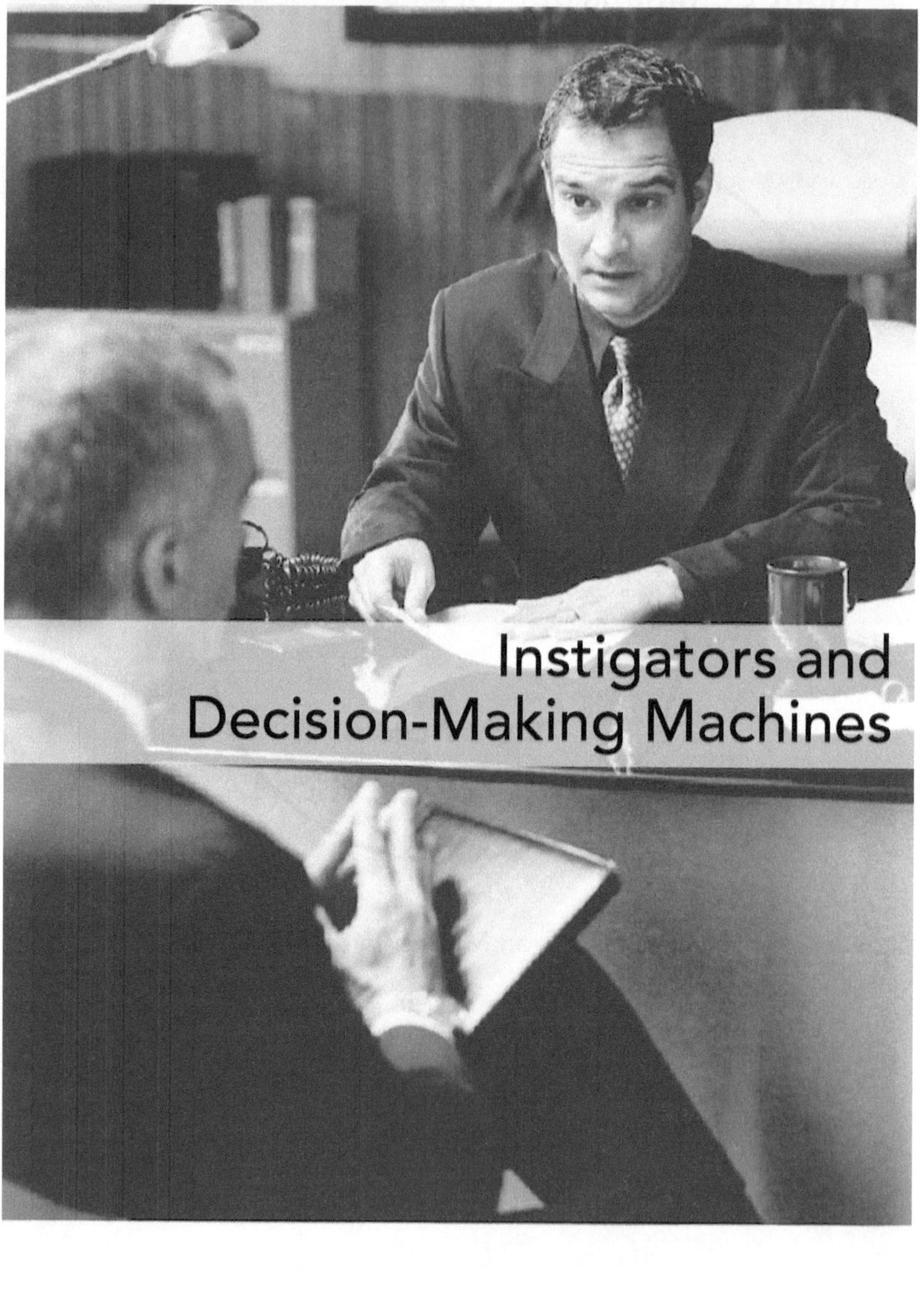

Chapter 4:
Decide, Discover, Deliver:
Instigators and
Decision-Making Machines

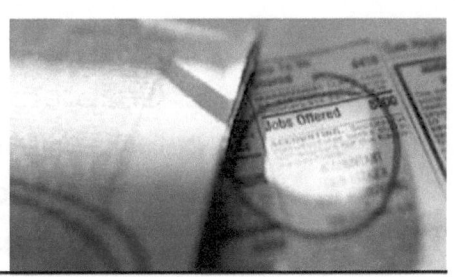

"This is your life
This is your day
Ain't no dress rehearsal
So get outta your way
Smell the roses
Dig the ride!
You can't take it with you when you say goodbye.

('cause) this is your life!"
—Joe Cocker "This is your Life" by
John Shanks and Shelly Peiken, *Respect Yourself*
Beacon Records, 2002.

DRESS REHEARSAL FOR DISASTER

Sam has been with Slumber, Inc. Pharmaceuticals for five years. His territory has been moderately successful. He has never been on warning and his boss generally leaves him alone. He knows his route cold and with the turnover his company has had, his new partners defer to him on most issues. He can set up an educational or promotional dinner program in the evenings and the "usual suspects" show up for the free food and camaraderie. He can get a lunch set up in a pinch whenever his District Sales Manager wants to see him in action in a big office. He never fails to get his expected 8-10 sample delivery "signatures" a day and knows where to drop the samples in every office in his territory. He's a valuable "employee."

It's Wednesday and Sam is hoping for an easy and short day. He knows he can get the required "signatures" to make it look like he put in a full day's activity. So he sets out on his route. It's a clear and crisp day and he hopes to really "dig the ride." His first call is brief, but friendly. The doctor asks "What's new?" Sam says, "not much, but my reports tell me that 'Pain-ex' prescriptions are doing well here. I just want to thank you for your support. I'll schedule a lunch so we can talk." The doctors

Chapter 4:
Decide, Discover, Deliver:
Instigators and
Decision-Making Machines

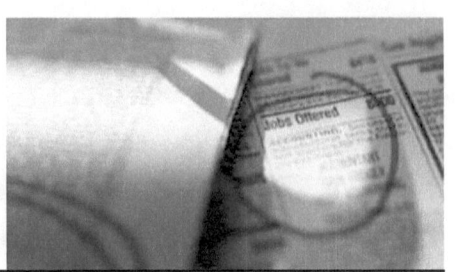

and nurses nod, smile, and leave him in the sample closet to fill the bins with his free drug.

Sam's entire morning pretty much mimics his first call. By 2 PM he's made his calls for the day. He rationalizes that if he makes more calls, he will go out of route for the day and run into his partners in other parts of the territory. Without calling any of them to double-check, he heads for the gym, then home for a great afternoon watching the first round of the Masters on cable. He DOES feel empty and even a bit guilty, but muses, "What are they going to do, fire me? I've paid my dues and have some great physician and pharmacist relationships. They can't afford to lose those!"

In today's world, Sam, the answer should be a definite and resounding "Don't bet on it!! It's time to brush up the resume!

Sam is on the road to becoming the rep who had the "easiest job he ever hated." The thrill is gone, the spirit is all dried up, the flare has fizzled. Talk about wasting "your life" and "your day." For Sam, his work day is a "dress rehearsal" for imminent disaster.

What Sam has NOT done is initiate action after making some critically WRONG decisions about his business.

DECISION-MAKING

With the increasing consolidation in the pharmaceutical industry, it's a whole new ballgame. Competition is fierce. Physician time is limited. The business does not run itself. Growth does not happen automatically. Companies can no longer achieve their sales goals by raising prices by 5% annually. Competitors are launching new products that are at least equal to if not better than yours. As a sales rep, you must make numerous

Chapter 4:

Decide, Discover, Deliver:
Instigators and Decision-Making Machines

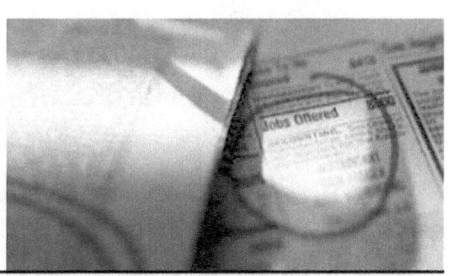

critical decisions daily. Time management lays the groundwork for your travels, but the call plan for each office also requires tactical decisions on the points you need to make on each call.

At this stage, the most important decision you as a candidate needs to make is whether you want to be just an "employee" like Sam, or as Tom Peters would describe, somebody who is constantly creating "Brand *You*" as opposed to being an anonymous "Brand X." (HAT'S OFF and Thanks to Tom for great metaphor!)

The critically wrong decisions drug reps make that flat-line their careers result from living in the "Employee" world, rather than the "Brand-You" World. Eventually, with the rising tide of new products (blip), new consolidated and strengthened sales forces in larger companies (bigger spLash!) and the lean and hungry District Sales Managers out there (crashing wave!) "good" employees like Sam will be washed away and rightfully so!

Here's my version of the Tom Peters list. A few items are borrowed directly from him. Later, we'll tie this in with some real-life decision-making scenarios to demonstrate my contentions. *It's "Brand you" or "Forget You!" in the Pharmaceutical field.*

Here is a comparison of the two realms and the activities probably under way in each of them:

"Brand You" Pharma World	*Pharma: Just an Employee"-World*
Developing a memorable (WOW) strategy. Focusing on a key group practice with all barrels blazing.	Calling on my target list daily.

Chapter 4:
Decide, Discover, Deliver:
Instigators and Decision-Making Machines

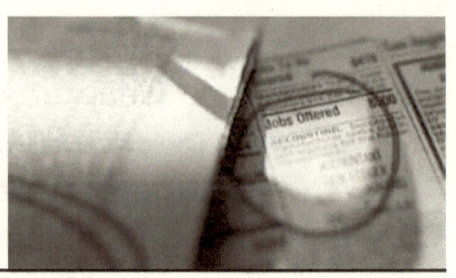

Committed to my craft. Intend to be incredibly good at the science of my drugs.

Working on cleaning out my information binder.

Debate with a resistant, stubborn doctor, because it will add to my learning, because it will s-t-r-e-t-c-h me/because it *may* someday pay off.

Call on him because my boss told me to. (Give me a break!)

Don't waste a single "lunch & learn" in a low-patient count office.

Have lunch with a friendly office. Socialize!

I AM A PDA (ROLODEX) MANIAC. I know everybody's name, pets names, Spouses name and birthday.

Don't try to push that BS off on me. They know why I'm there.

Understand that "Sales-Goals-Are-Me." Period. I *am* my drug "portfolio."

I show up. I don't make waves.

Love the words: WOW Beauty . . . Grace . . . Revolution . . . Impact.

Oh, grow up!

L-i-v-e for my clients!

I do my job.

Purposefully hang out with the movers and shakers.

My pals are my pals.
My pals are my pals.
Lay off.

My work is "fun"—cool.

C'mon! A day at work is a day at work.

Am anxious to get out of bed in the morning.	Sleep in! The offices Don't open until 9!
Am in the hospital parking lot at 7:00 when the docs are finishing morning patient rounds.	
Would love to have been with Washington at Valley Forge!	I'm almost vested. Don't Tread on me.
Love bright colors!	Gray is beautiful.
I communicate pro-actively.	I AM AN EMAIL MAN!
Embrace life.	Don't work a minute past 5!
It's better to ask forgiveness than beg for permission (Always!)	Don't expose your butt. (CYA)

Mark my words. Half of YOU will end up in the "Employee" mode in about three years if you are not Instigators and Decision-Making Machines.

Sam has not made a decision in weeks, other than to decide what he will watch on TV when he gets home early. Decision making in the pharmaceutical business involves comparing data from many sources to determine courses of action, and then taking action that is based upon facts.

DECISION-MAKING TOOLBOX

In the last chapter we talked about target lists and data. It is a well known fact that the pharmaceutical industry purchases prescribing data for use in guiding its sales force. For trend analysis, this information is solid. *"Employees"* would rather dispute the data and keep hanging

Chapter 4:

Decide, Discover, Deliver:
Instigators and
Decision-Making Machines

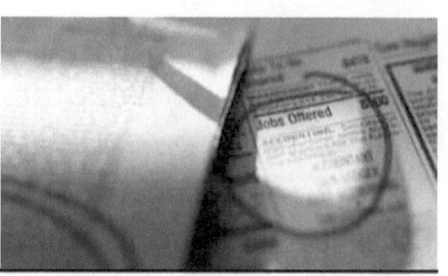

with their "friends" than pursue difficult but high-volume medical practices or sharpen their messages and "closes" on the physicians who are resistant, or worse, on-board but slipping away.

Instead of gathering information, interpreting the data, generating alternative approaches, choosing new courses of action, or involving their partners in the issues they have uncovered, they GO HOME EARLY!!!

Let's take a look at three scenarios to see what you are most likely to do. Be honest with yourself. We're talking about your career and life here!

1. Here's one really close to home. What type of information have you used in your career search decisions? Have you used any real data? What have you read? Has your opinion changed as the result of research? What is the result so far?

2. Describe a difficult decision you recently had to make. What factors did you consider? How long did it take to make a decision?

3. Pharmaceutical Scenario: A key prescriber ran into you in the hospital hallway this morning and said "I need to see you this afternoon. PLEASE come by the office at about 5:45." No explanation. You have an early dinner date that evening with a nurse you met last week. You can't image what the doctor could want, since he usually is a "no-see" to you. What do you do? (Tons of options here for decisions *and* preparations for action.)

These are tough questions to answer honestly if you are on the "Employee" side of the list above. For the "Brand You" person, they are easy.

Chapter 4:

Decide, Discover, Deliver:
Instigators and
Decision-Making Machines

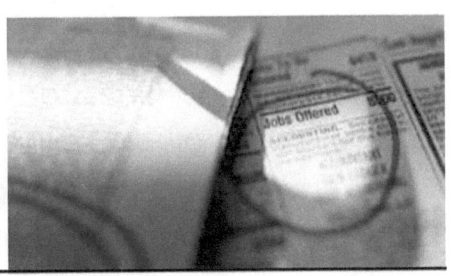

THE PASSION OF AN INITIATOR

Forget Sam! His company will have forgotten him long before he is vested. The successful rep takes action quickly, and does it independently, going beyond what is expected by clients, partners, and managers. As leader of a well-prepared team, the top notch rep knows what his manager's and partners' reactions will be to initiative—time is a commodity not to be wasted.

Here are additional scenarios to see if you have the Abilities to be a Decision-Making Machine.

1. What have you changed about your *current* job? Why did you make these changes? What was the result?

2. Describe one time when you did a LOT more than what was required. What happened?

3. Pharmaceutical Scenario. Your team is simply "tapped out." You've been floundering for about six months. One of your best prescribers dies unexpectedly. The dominant Managed Care plan in your area has taken your drug off their Preferred Drug List. (It's still available if the physician calls in a "Prior Authorization" to the insurance company.) One of your partners is on a third interview with a competitor. IT JUST CAN'T GO ON LIKE THIS!!! What do you do?

REMEMBER, THIS CHAPTER IS ABOUT DECISION-MAKING AND TAKING INITIATIVE.

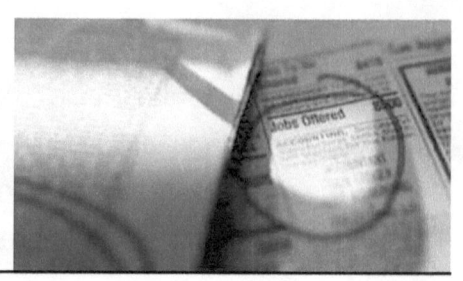

Chapter 4:

Decide, Discover, Deliver:
Instigators and
Decision-Making Machines

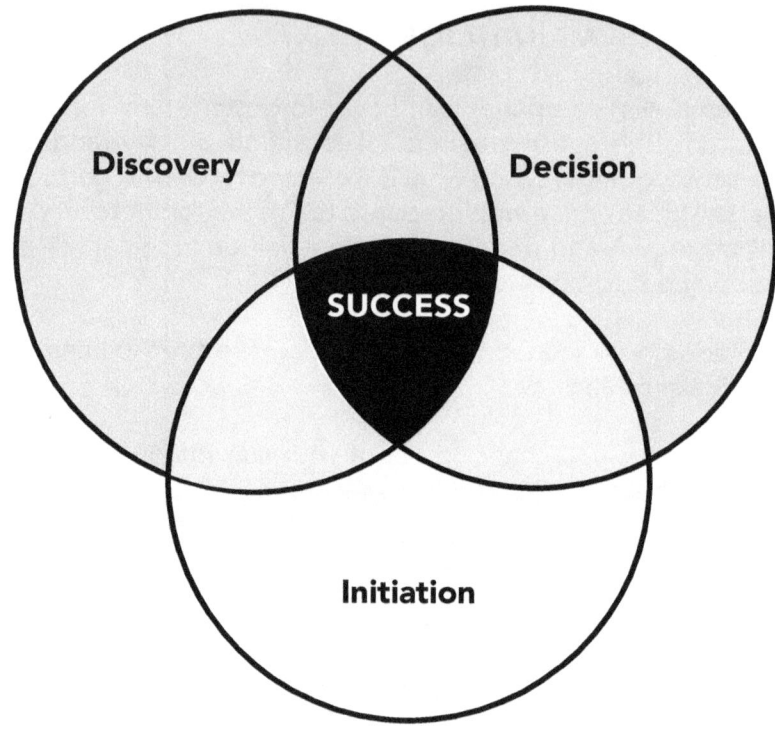

Next we hit the technical stuff. Hope you're still with me.

Technical Ability, Professional Knowledge, On-Going Learning

Chapter 5:
Is Your Hair on Fire?
Technical Ability,
Professional Understanding,
Continuous Learning

Sri Ramakrishna said:

"Do not seek illumination
unless you seek it
as a man whose hair is on fire
seeks a pond."

How many science majors did you hang out with in college? How many do you even know? How many registered nurses, physicians, rehab therapists, dentists are there in your family? For many the answer is "None!" Were you a science major? Probably not. Does that mean you don't have the GENIUS compatible with selling pharmaceuticals? Not necessarily. In fact, you CAN develop the ABILITY to use technical data to sell pharmaceuticals effectively.

Understanding and USING Technical Knowledge.

Once again, as with all other ABILITIES, a facility with technical information *can* be attained and developed.

The best and most accessible test of your ABILITY is to attempt to read the *Detailed Prescribing Information* (DPI) available for just about any drug from just about any Pharmacist. Your doctor also receives samples from drug representatives daily and with each sample the DPI must also be attached. Ask your pharmacist or doctor to get you one for a drug you may be taking. Ask the doc's receptionist to give you one from the sample closet "DETAILING" a NEW blockbuster drug. READ IT. Attempt to explain to your best friend, or yourself in the mirror. I'd suggest comparing what the DPI says with what the commercials purport to be the value of the product. Look for these factors:

Chapter 5:
Is Your Hair on Fire?
Technical Ability, Professional Understanding, Continuous Learning

1. Indications
2. Pharmacology
3. Dosage and Administration
4. Side Effects
5. Warnings

If you can SPEAK on the basics of these five topics with STYLE after two or three readings, you can probably begin to do the job of a pharmaceutical representative.

Another tool used in selling is the Clinical Trial. Data is constantly amassed on drugs. Before a drug is launched it goes through three phases of testing, which ultimately include large-scale efficacy and safety trials that are published in medical journals. After a drug is launched, companies conduct long-term post-marketing (called Phase Four) evaluations, more specific trials for marketing purposes, and trials to gain new indications (i.e. approved prescribing uses.)

Just for fun, go to one of the following journals or their websites and read one of the latest trials published:

> JAMA (Journal of the American Medical Association)
> Archives of Internal Medicine
> NEJM (New England journal of Medicine)

(You can find these and other journals at <medscape.com> or at a Medical Library.)

Go ahead, I dare you!

Here's why it is critically important that you learn to present clinical and scientific data. Think of it this way. You wake up one morning and your

car is running rough. It lurches, snorts and grumbles all the way to your local mechanic. You ask him to fix it. At the end of the day, he bills you $400. You exhibit signs of disbelief and distress. "My car was running fine yesterday!"

Imagine your dismay when he replies, "Well, ya know, the whatchamacallit was busted, and that ain't easy to fix. YOU KNOW what I mean. This stuff happens, but I know it's fixed."

If that's the best he can do, will you pay willingly? Will you go back to that garage? Will you listen to every sound your car makes for weeks? OK, that's the point. You have to gain credibility and be able to answer questions about your products, their indications, dosage, side effects and cost. Remember the "undifferentiated market" discussion from Chapter Two! A smile, chocolate, and donuts will NOT increase your market share—and that's increasingly how your incentives are paid.

If you cannot use scientific data convincingly to win the war for prescriptions, you will not succeed. You will become at best a hard-working sample-dropper, donut buyer, or candy deliverer, who goes home every night wondering what today was all about.

SOME TECHNICAL KNOWLEDGE SCENARIOS.

OK! So you've done all of the little projects I just described and you are becoming even more enthused. You have the ABILITY. In fact, you felt quite proud when you spoke to the man (or woman) in the mirror. You now feel like this type of thing is part of your GENIUS that had just not come to the surface until now. The unanswered question relates to the "P" word. Your PASSION. How do the ones you outlined in Chapter One relate to this new experience? Will you be happy and fulfilled for the rest of your career dealing with this data.

Chapter 5:
Is Your Hair on Fire?
Technical Ability, Professional Understanding, Continuous Learning

Let's do some exercises investigating your past life to see if this new PASSION will be sustained over time. Take a look at these scenarios. Once again, evaluate your responses and how you FEEL about these situations from your current profession or personal life.

1. In your current position, have you ever had to train a new employee on a technical task or area of activity? (e.g. what makes the copy machine tick, how to meter mail, how to work their PDA to be more than a calendar, etc.) Talk about those situations. How did you teach them? What theoretical and practical information did you use? What was the result?

2. What was the most complex technical assignment you ever worked on? What was your responsibility? What did you learn from it? How did you master the material?

3. A group of Physicians and Residents at your major hospital have what's called a "Journal Club" every month at which they discuss recent journal articles relevant to their area of specialization? Where would you go to find suitable articles? Can you start on the internet? Try putting together a program with recent articles from JAMA, NEJM and others on Ulcer treatment.

Rest assured that in your basic training with any pharmaceutical company you will receive instruction on Medical Terminology, Clinical Pharmacology, and the Anatomy and Physiology relating to the products you will be selling. Your confidence in your newly-discovered ABILITY will grow, and grow, and grow.

Chapter 5:
Is Your Hair on Fire?
Technical Ability,
Professional Understanding,
Continuous Learning

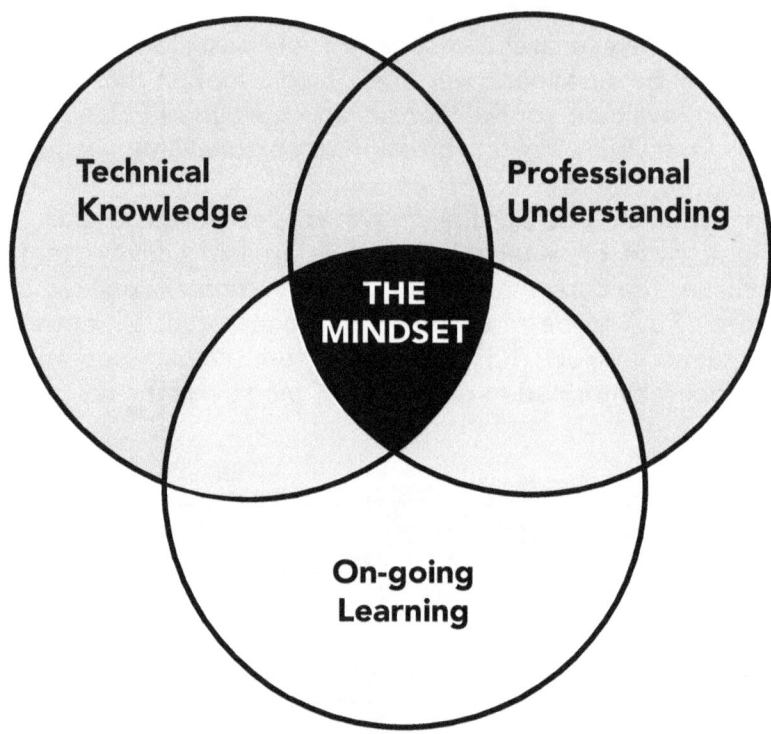

Are you committed "to the marrow" to continued self-improvement?

What was the last book you read? Was it fiction or non-fiction? Did you finish it? What was the theme? What will you read next?

What was the last course you took on your own *after* graduating from college? Do you listen to books on tape? Do you belong to a book club?

Do you have a hobby? What magazines do you read in connection with this avocation of yours?

Chapter 5:
Is Your Hair on Fire?
Technical Ability, Professional Understanding, Continuous Learning

In short, do you exercise your brain every day? If you cannot accumulate any evidence that you do, you're not even in the ball park.

Dedicated and serious pharmaceutical sales reps immerse themselves in information. They see it everywhere and investigate it.

A COMFORTING NOTE ON CONTINUOUS LEARNING

To continue with car analogies, let's say you've been in the market for a long time and after a great deal of deliberation, decide to buy a Volvo. You're worried about your choice, since nobody in your family has one, they are relatively expensive, and the cost of maintenance is a bit higher than domestic cars. All in all, you're questioning your decision—classic buyer's remorse.

As you drive down the highway, you start to look around and "Whoa! There's a Volvo ahead." And "Hey, here comes another one in the oncoming lane." And again and again and again. All of a sudden it's RAINING VOLVOS!

The reason for this is that your mind has been sensitized to seek out Volvos in order to calm your anxieties. The same is true of Medical and Scientific information. As you become involved in the pharmaceutical industry, and your livelihood depends upon your knowledge and ability to transmit it in a persuasive way, you will be flooded with new data every day. To succeed, you have to evaluate it all and USE it in your presentations.

Remember, the patients who call on your physicians are also sensitized to receive information about their condition and the drugs they take to treat it. They believe innacurate information in the media reports, rumors heard in the barber shop or beauty salon, or misinterpretations by their friends. Then they bombard their doctor or his/her nurse about these rumors, inaccuracies and lies.

You have to prepare your customers to answer these questions that are based upon information that is out there every day. If you're like the infamous Sam, getting through his day as an "employee," you will be frustrated, angered, dismayed. You will surely *fail* in this position.

One more challenge. Do an Internet search using the keywords "Arthritis" and "Treatment" or "Depression" or "Allergies." Read the best twenty articles you can find in the lay press. Save them in a file and keep on reading them. Who knows, they may help you on an interview someday soon.

Think about it!

Greatness: Tenacity, Adaptability, Resiliency

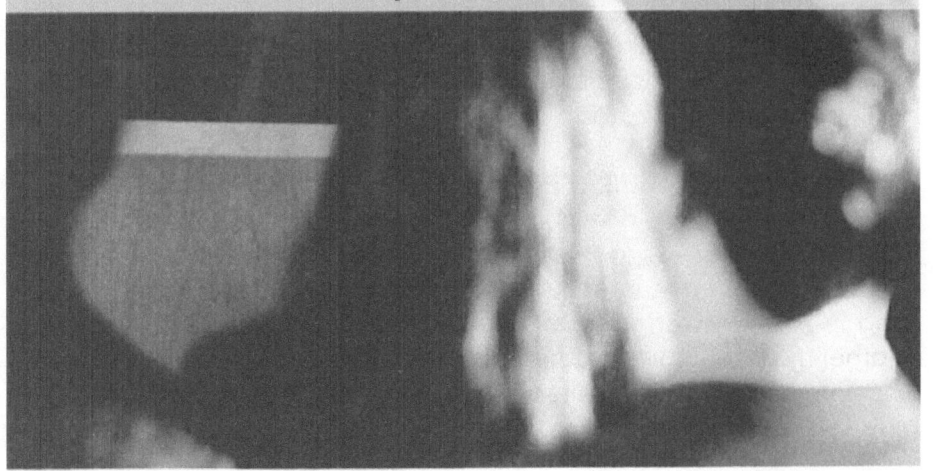

Chapter 6:
Greatness:
Tenacity, Adaptability,
Resiliency

In Chapter Five, we discussed ABILITIES that for the most part can be *learned*. Many hiring managers argue that they interview for information about things that *cannot* be taught or learned. They are looking for the innate qualities i.e. GENIUS that will make a candidate successful.

Until recently, few writers have convincingly emphasized the simple term "GREAT" in discussing businesses—even less so as regards everyday PEOPLE pursuing careers. (If you don't trust me, use the web and do a word search on the keyword GREATNESS; you'll be convinced.) That all changed with Jim Collins' wonderful book *Good to Great*, published in 2001. If UNGLAMOROUS but determined *companies* can aspire to greatness, so can *individuals* who work for them.

Second point. The aphorism "Some men are born great; other's have greatness thrust upon them" certainly applies here. While the GENIUS aspects of tenacity, adaptability and resiliency cannot be CONSCIOUSLY learned, they can be "thrust upon you." If you've had serious life changes happen already, (I suspect you have or you would not be working on this book) it will surface in your conversations, interviews, and reactions to situations during the hiring and education process. Let's consider each of these:

THE TWIN MONSTERS "TENACITY" AND "ADAPTABILITY"

Classical Literature enthusiasts might consider these two as the "Scylla and Charybidis" of career success. In the Greek mythology Charybdis lived in a cave at one end of the Strait of Messina, directly opposite another monster, Scylla. Both monsters were constant threats to passing ships. In modern terms, sailors were between "the devil and the deep blue sea" or between "the rock and the hard place."

For many personalities, tenacity and adaptability are the Scylla and Charybdis threatening their career advancement. At healthy levels, they are necessary assets, but tenacity often becomes stubbornness

Chapter 6:
Greatness:
Tenacity, Adaptability,
Resiliency

or counter-productive bullheadedness. Adaptability can become a lack of will or even laziness and is certainly perceived as a lack of commitment.

Tenacity and adaptability seem contradictory, but life is filled with this sort of duality—body and soul, intelligence and emotion, love and hate etc. In maturity, many begin to recognize that such apparent dualities are not opposites, *but two sides of the same coin.*

As you do the exercises below, however, you'll see that tenacity and adaptability relate in just this way, and their combination can result in an unbeatable Resiliency. With Resiliency as a resulting GENIUS you didn't "know" was yours—you're on your way to GREATNESS.

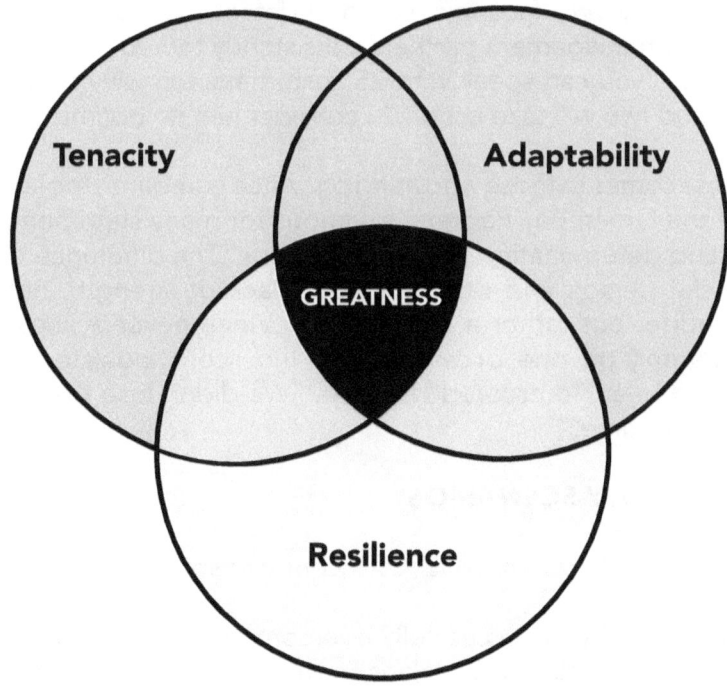

Chapter 6:
Greatness:
Tenacity, Adaptability,
Resiliency

PORTRAITS OF TENACITY

Let's look at some "overnight successes" familiar to us all. One of the most famous is Thomas Edison who clearly lightened and brightened all of our lives. It is a well-known fact that Edison had countless failures on the way to producing the light bulb. His two famous comments indicate what the trait Tenacity is all about. Said Edison, commenting on creative frustration—"I have not failed. I've just found 10,000 ways that won't work." In the face of setbacks, the great inventor also said that "Opportunity is missed by most people because it is dressed in overalls and looks like work." And perhaps his most famous statement—"Genius is one percent inspiration and 99% perspiration."

As a pharmaceutical rep in today's highly competitive and restrictive environment, you will face rejection and defeat *most* of the time. One of my former management partners consistently touted his "25-10-5-2" rule. That is, "you can speak with 25 customers, ten will listen, five will respond, and two will take action." I consider him an *optimist*.

But success comes to those who hang on. Vince Lombardi, the legendary coach of the Green Bay Packers, is famous for many statements about tenacity and determination. Two favorites are "The difference between a successful person and others is not a lack of strength, not a lack of knowledge, but rather a lack of will." Vince never acknowledged defeat. Rather, on one occasion after the score indicated that the Packers had been "outscored" he said, "We didn't lose the game; we just ran out of time."

SOME TENACITY SCENARIOS

That's Tenacity! Do *you* have it? Let's consider some scenarios.

1. When did you successfully overcome objections to show how your products (ideas, plans, requests) met the needs of your

Chapter 6:
Greatness:
Tenacity, Adaptability, Resiliency

customer (spouse, parents, professors)? Describe the situation. What did you do? What did you gain?

2. Talk about a time when you submitted a good idea to your boss (wife, parents, professors) and were shot down. What did you do? What did you gain?

3. Pharmaceutical Scenario. You've just made a FANTASTIC, MIND-BLOWING presentation to your top physician. She seemed interested and engaged throughout. When you "closed" for the business, she said. "No! I'm still not convinced. (READ: I'm not about to *change the way I practice medicine*.) What will you do? THIS IS CRITICAL, BECAUSE WHETHER THEY SAY "NO" OR NOT, THIS IS WHAT THEY ARE THINKING—95% OF THE TIME!!

Tenacity is not beating your head against the wall, especially if the wall is not the one you want to break through ANYWAY. Tenacity is best described as the experience of a lost hiker hiker running through the woods at night. His nose encounters a tree, but in desperation, he bobs to the left and continues to run until the next encounter, then bobs to the right, and runs on, and the "bang" another tree. To reach his goal, the errant woodsman runs until he is out of the woods. That's tenacity BEING THRUST UPON YOU! In sales, most of your days will match the experience of this lost hiker—rejection after rejection compounded by insincere promises and many a casual "sure I'll do that." But when you reach the light of day and your market share jumps—the joy and rewards are great.

Chapter 6:
Greatness:
Tenacity, Adaptability,
Resiliency

MORE ABOUT THE OTHER MONSTER—ADAPTABILITY

The pace of change accelerates constantly. Not only is change continual, but it's gaining speed at an incremental rate. Change impacts all aspects of the job.

Your Company. You can almost say that every day is a brand new day. It's not uncommon for Pharmaceutical Reps with 5-10 years experience to have gone through three mergers or acquisitions in which their companies changed hands. If they're with a "winner," they've launched a new drug at least once every 18 months. It's also common to have a new boss (District Sales Manager) every year. Their territories are re-aligned with each of these launches as company analysts make sure the market is covered in each medical subspecialty with, ONCE AGAIN, the right message going to the right physicians with the right frequency.

The Managed Care/Insurance Environment. In the world of Managed Care, formularies (i.e. lists of approved drugs covered with varying patient co-pays) change at least annually. As a primary care representative, you will have to be familiar with these issues and guide your customers through the labyrinth of prior authorizations, tiered co-pays, preferred drug lists and obstinate pharmacists to help them get the drugs they want (yours) for their patients. Prescribers are understandably frustrated by this constant maze. You have to be adaptable to guide them out of the forest.

Let's look at some Adaptability scenarios from your past and possibly future life.

1. We've all had to make changes when the way we've been doing things is no longer effective. When was the last time you tried a new approach to a task, problem, assignment, relationship? What did you do? What were the results?

Chapter 6:
Greatness:
Tenacity, Adaptability,
Resiliency

2. Discuss a situation in which you had to adjust quickly to a significant change in the organization, department, or team priorities. How did the change affect you? What did you do?

3. Pharmaceutical Sales scenario. You've just learned that there is to be a re-organization in your company. Your District Sales Manager and his boss, the Regional Sales Director, have both been given new assignments. You are also in the midst of a product launch and will be assigned to a new DSM who is known to be a real "_____buster." How will you react? What will you do to regain control of your life? What will your first communication be?

Are you Resilient?

In sales you will face rejection. You will not gain a market share of 100%, although that should be your goal. What can you do to come close?

1. Persist in finding a way to see the right physicians. Be tenacious. If their offices are closed to you, find out when they come to work. Approach them in the parking lot, hallway, or hospital cafeteria. Be visible to them in their environment and strike up a conversation. Get the ball rolling in that way. Learn about their hobbies or interests from their receptionist, office nurse, or office manager. Use that information to strike up a conversation. You will set your self apart from the competition by even trying.

2. Adapt your approach to the doctor's personality. You can present your core message in many ways to different personality types. Is your customer an analytical type who wants more and more data? You WILL have it to present. Is he/she moved by emotion and conviction? Turn it on! Is the target an amiable personality?

Chapter 6:
Greatness:
Tenacity, Adaptability,
Resiliency

Ask him to help you understand how to present the results of a new clinical trial your company has published. Is the doctor a person who has a large ego and loves to be praised? Make her feel important. Ask her if you can discuss their successes with your products with their peers. Let her know you think of her as a thought leader in the medical community. Adapt!

3. Call on your doctors with the right frequency. Sell them again, and again, and again. Adapt your message not just to their personalities, but also to the needs of their individual practice and the types of patients they treat.

The rewards of the resiliency born of tenacity and adaptability are great!

Conclusion and Self-Test

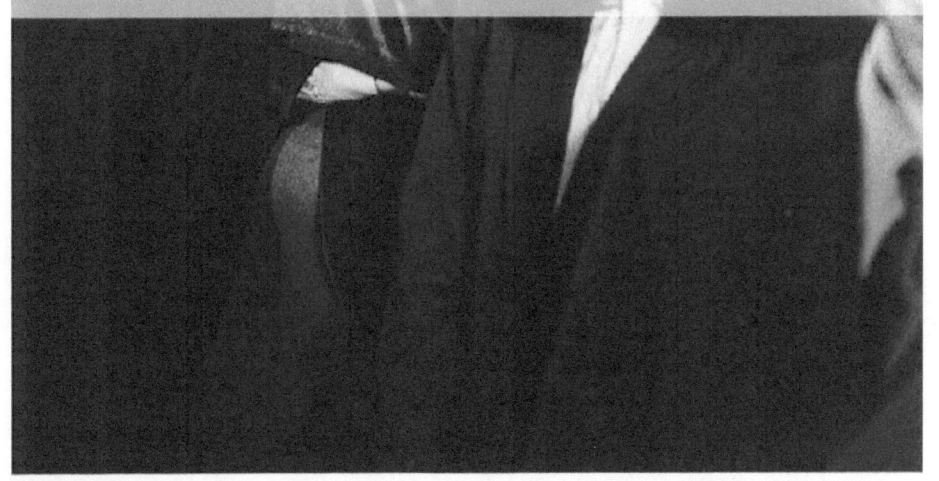

Conclusion and Self-Test

What is the conclusion?

I don't know. Is Pharmaceutical Sales Right for YOU? You can probably answer that question now. If you are convinced that your GENIUS is right for Pharmaceutical Sales, and you have the ABILITY to execute the basic functions of the job, what remains is the most critical question. Do you have a PASSION for this line of work?

If despite the downsides I've fairly presented you are even MORE inspired than before to explore this field—GREAT, CONTACT US.

First take a look at this summary quiz. Send us your score if you would like to and let's discuss your GENIUS, ABILITIES, AND PASSIONS. We welcome the chance to help you launch a great career.

Review your answers to the scenarios presented in each preceding chapter. Pick the answer most closely resembling yours.

Here goes!

1. The doctor NEVER sees drug reps, but one is there now?
   a. Say thanks and walk out.
   b. Mention the rep you can both see and ask for an appointment as soon as possible.
   c. Talk to the receptionist about the merits of your product while inquiring about the type of patients most often treated in the office.

2. Dr. Patel never prescribes a drug until it is on the market for one year.
   a. Tell Dr. Patel your drug has actually been on the market for two years.

   b. Remind Dr. Patel of the disadvantages of other currently available drugs.

   c. Provide Dr. Patel with a third party endorsement from one of his peers or a recognized expert in his specialty.

3. The wrong dosing scenario.
   a. Thank the doctor for doubling your sales by doubling the dose.
   b. Point out the correct dose in the Package Insert.
   c. Show efficacy comparisons of your drug and competitors at the proper dose.

4. The docs don't show up for your big lunch.
   a. Put the lunch back in your trunk and leave.
   b. Leave the lunch for the office staff and go to a different office.
   c. Stay and sell to everybody in the office, outlining the merits of your product and asking the staff to explain its relevance to their practice.

5. Dr. Cassandra only wants to see *you*.
   a. Tell your boss about the problem and let him sort it out.
   b. Discuss the situation at your next meeting with your partners.
   c. Meet the customers needs for all your company's products after working out a strategy with both management and your peers.

6. The 5:45 meeting, or the date?
   a. Tell the doctor you can't make it.
   b. Show up; move your date back an hour.
   c. Go to the office early; ask the office staff what the issue might be.

7. The team and you are "tapped out."
   a. Call another rep and moan.
   b. Call Human Resources.
   c. Call your District Sales Manager and ask for advice.

8. The "Journal Club". How many articles did you find?
   a. None
   b. Two
   c. Three or more

9. Doctor is still not convinced.
   a. You say, "OK, what about my other products?"
   b. You find out what competing product the doctor likes to use.
   c. You probe for the real objection until you get it.

10. The reorganization and new boss.
    a. Call another rep to moan (again).
    b. Call your partners to a meeting.
    c. Call your prior manager to get advice on how to use your strengths to got off to a new start.

Here's the scoring (if it isn't obvious). The "a's" equal—1. the "b's" equal "0" and the "c's" equal a +1. If you scored above an "8" start your job search today.

SOME STEPS TO START YOUR SEARCH

It would require a separate workbook to outline success stories of candidates who interviewed well and landed the job. That being said, here are some very basic tips to get you started.

Most companies DO actually rely upon their websites to find candidates. Contact them and watch their websites for weekly updates. You can

Conclusion and Self-Test

normally post for many jobs in this way once you have done the initial application needed to be considered.

Spend time with your resume prepared in the hallways of medical office buildings. Start up conversations with representatives you meet there. Most companies have an Employee Referral Program which rewards representatives for referring candidates who are hired.

Check out the sites of major Recruiting Process Outsourcing (RPO) companies like my alma mater Inventivhealth. In today's market, more and more pharmaceutical companies, large and small, are using the services of RPO's to augment and even replace their own recruiting operations.

Watch websites like Monster.com, Careerbuilder, and Medzilla for notices of sales-oriented job fairs or hiring events in your area and by all means attend them.

Ask the staff in your doctor's office about their best reps and ask for their contact information, business cards, or email addresses. Of course, contact them about your interest.

Once you begin the process, you will no doubt find even more creative ways to network a resume into a "face-to-face" interview.

You should be confident that you are now well prepared!

Best of luck in your career change!

Acknowledgements and
Further Reading

Acknowledgements & Further Reading

I highly recommend the following books.

John P. Kotter, *Leading Change*. Harvard Business School Press (Boston, 1996)

John C. Maxwell. *The 21 Indispensable Qualities of a Leader: Becoming the Person Others will Want to Follow*. Thomas Nelson Publishers (*Nashville, 1999*)

Tom Peters. *Thriving on Chaos: Handbook for a Management Revolution*. Alfred A. Knopf, (NY 1987)

Tom Peters. *The Work Matters*. available at <tompeters.com>

Marcus Buckingham and Curt Coffman, *First, Break All the Rules: What the World's Greatest Managers do Differently*. Simon & Schuster (New York, 1999)

James C. Collins and Jerry I. Porras, *Built to Last: Successful Habits of Visionary Companies*, Harper Business (New York, 1994)

Jim Collins, *Good to Great*. Harper Business (New York, 2001)

Jack Mitchell, *Hug Your Customers; the Proven Way to Personalize Sales and Achieve Outstanding Results*. Hyperion Books (New York, 2003)

Rick Pitino (with Bill Reynolds), *Success is a Choice: Ten Steps to Overachieve in Business and Life*. Broadway Books (New York 1997)

The ultimate and most monumental "thank you" goes to my wonderful wife Ilona for her encouragement and partnership throughout this writing process.

www.ingramcontent.com/pod-product-compliance
Lightning Source LLC
Chambersburg PA
CBHW021903170526
45157CB00005B/1942